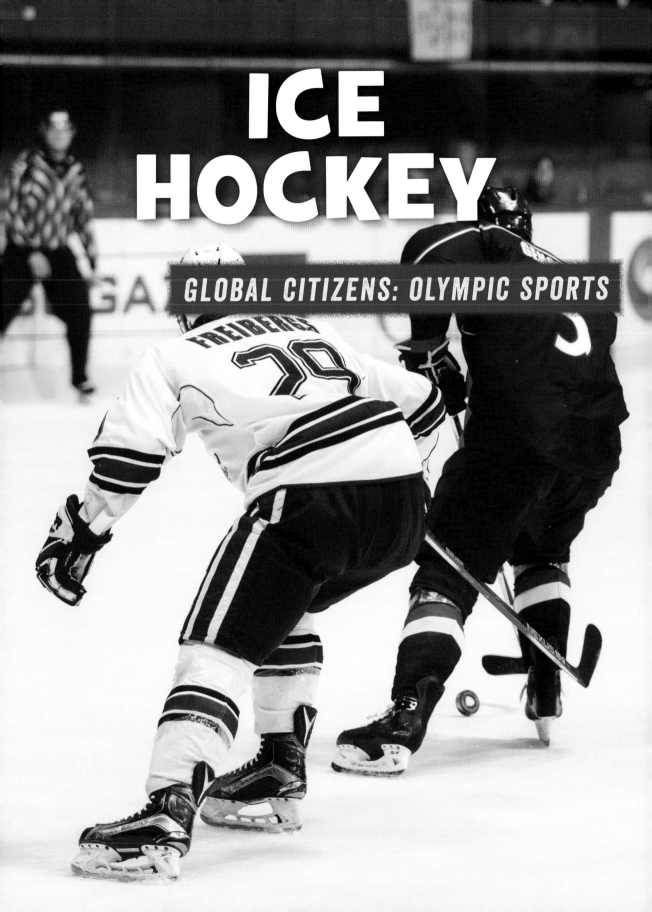

ICE
HOCKEY

GLOBAL CITIZENS: OLYMPIC SPORTS

Published in the United States of America by Cherry Lake Publishing
Ann Arbor, Michigan
www.cherrylakepublishing.com

Content Adviser: Liv Williams, Editor, www.iLivExtreme.com
Reading Adviser: Marla Conn MS, Ed., Literacy specialist, Read-Ability, Inc.

Photo Credits: ©Ivica Drusany / Shutterstock.com, cover; Nationaal Archief / flickr.com, 5; ©Alison Young / Shutterstock.com, 7; ©KUCO / Shutterstock.com, 8; ©Iurii Osadchi / Shutterstock.com, 11, 12, 21; ©Chase N. / flickr.com, 13; ©Pukhov K / Shutterstock.com, 14; ©Peter Vanderheyden / flickr.com, 16; ©Kvanta / Shutterstock.com, 19; ©rook76 / Shutterstock.com, 22; ©Daniel M. Silva / Shutterstock.com, 24; ©Sergei Bachlakov / Shutterstock.com, 27; ©Mitrofanov Alexander / Shutterstock.com, 28

Library of Congress Cataloging-in-Publication Data

Names: Labrecque, Ellen, author.
Title: Ice hockey / by Ellen Labrecque.
Description: Ann Arbor, Michigan : Cherry Lake Publishing, 2018. | Series: Global citizens: Olympic sports |
    Includes bibliographical references and index.
Identifiers: LCCN 2017029644 | ISBN 9781534107526 (hardcover) | ISBN 9781534109506 (pdf) |
    ISBN 9781534108516 (pbk.) | ISBN 9781534120495 (hosted ebook)
Subjects: LCSH: Hockey—Juvenile literature. | Winter Olympics—Juvenile literature.
Classification: LCC GV847.25 .L335 2018 | DDC 796.962—dc23
LC record available at https://lccn.loc.gov/2017029644

Cherry Lake Publishing would like to acknowledge the work of The Partnership for 21st Century Learning.
Please visit *www.p21.org* for more information.

Printed in the United States of America
Corporate Graphics

ABOUT THE AUTHOR

Ellen Labrecque has written over 100 books for children. She loves the Olympics and has attended both the Winter and Summer Games as a reporter for magazines and television. She lives in Yardley, Pennsylvania, with her husband, Jeff, and her two young "editors," Sam and Juliet. When she isn't writing, she is running, hiking, and reading.

TABLE OF CONTENTS

CHAPTER 1

2## History: Ice Hockey 4

CHAPTER 2

Geography: Go North,
Ice Hockey Players! 10

CHAPTER 3

Civics: Olympic Pride 18

CHAPTER 4

Economics: Ice Hockey
Is Big Business 26

THINK ABOUT IT.. 30
FOR MORE INFORMATION.. 31
GLOSSARY 32
INDEX 32

History: Ice Hockey

The first Winter Olympics was held in Chamonix, France, from January 25 to February 5, 1924. It included 258 athletes from 16 different countries competing in 16 events. Since then, the Winter Olympics has been held every 4 years in a number of countries. (The Games were skipped in 1940 and 1944 during World War II.) As the Games progressed, more competitors and events were added. Fast-forward to the 2014 Winter Games held in Sochi, Russia. There were 2,873 competitors from 88 different countries competing in 98 events. That's a lot more competitors and events!

Men's ice hockey made its Winter Olympic debut at the 1924 Games.

From jaw-dropping aerial flips in snowboarding to the graceful choreography of figure skating, the Winter Games display some of the most unbelievable sports and athletes. Tickets to the Olympic ice hockey games have almost always been among the hardest to get. It's no wonder—everybody wants to watch this thrilling and action-packed sport!

The Story of Ice Hockey

Ice hockey was included in the first Winter Olympics in 1924. Surprisingly, it was also included in the Summer Olympics 4 years earlier. But only the men's teams competed. The women's teams were later added to the Olympics at the 1998 Winter Games in Nagano, Japan.

Ice hockey is the national sport of Canada. It is also the sport's birthplace. The word *hockey* comes from the French word *hoquet*, which means "shepherd's crook." This refers to the shape of the hockey stick. Many different parts of Canada (including Nova Scotia and Ontario) claim to be the place the sport started, but nobody can say this for sure. What is known is that the first organized game of ice hockey was played at McGill University in Montreal, Quebec, in 1875. J.G.A. Creighton, a McGill student, created the first set of rules. The players used a wooden **puck**, as opposed to a ball used in other stick games. The puck was less likely to bounce up and injure players and fans.

In 1877, the McGill University Hockey Club became the first organized team. After that, the sport quickly took off across Canada. In 1890, the Ontario Hockey Association was formed

The Hockey Hall of Fame in Toronto, Canada, houses the first Stanley Cup trophy.

and included colleges, universities, and other athletic club teams. A competition would be held every year to determine which team was the best. In 1893, Governor General Lord Stanley donated a trophy for the winner of the competition. The first Stanley Cup game was played on March 22 of that same year. Ever since the National Hockey League (NHL) was formed in 1917, the Stanley Cup has gone to the winner of the NHL **playoffs**.

When ice hockey was included in the 1920 Olympics, Canada easily won the gold, defeating the United States.

Early Czechoslovakian ice hockey was called "bandy hokej" and was played slightly differently from the Canadian game.

Olympic Ice Hockey Today

At first, **professional** ice hockey players were not supposed to play in the Olympics. The players had to be **amateurs**. But some countries, like the Soviet Union and Czechoslovakia, paid their players. Since it was the government paying them and not a league like the NHL, these players were still considered amateurs. This put these countries at an advantage. The International

Olympic Committee (IOC) finally decided to change this rule and allowed all players, including the paid ones, to play. At the 1998 Olympics in Nagano, Japan, professional players competed in the Olympics for the first time. However, as of 2018, the NHL has decided to reverse this rule and not let their players compete in the Games.

Developing Claims and Using Evidence

In many Olympic sports, it takes a lot longer for women to get a chance to compete. In the case of ice hockey, women didn't get an opportunity until 78 years after the first time men competed for Olympic glory. Why do you think that women didn't get to start at the same time as men? Use the data you find from the Internet and your local library to support your argument.

CHAPTER 2

Geography: Go North, Ice Hockey Players!

Currently, 76 countries in the world have a men's national ice hockey team and 51 have a women's national team. At the 2014 Winter Olympics, there were 12 men's teams and eight women's teams competing for an Olympic medal. In the entire world, close to 2 million people play organized ice hockey. Leading the way are Canada (over 600,000 people play) and the United States (over 500,000 people play).

So where do the best ice hockey players in the world come from? Which countries have won the most Olympic ice hockey medals?

The US women's ice hockey team brought home silver at the 2014 Sochi Games.

The Canadian women's ice hockey team defeated the US team for gold in overtime at the 2014 Games.

Canada

Canada has won more medals, including more gold medals, than any other country in ice hockey at the Winter Olympics. The men have won 15 medals total, including nine gold. On the women's side, Canada has won five medals, including four gold.

The men's team dominated in the early years from 1920 to 1952, winning six gold medals and one silver. Similarly, when the women's team officially entered the Games in 1998, they consistently brought home gold for every Olympic ice hockey

Canada beat Russia (pictured) in the quarterfinals at the 2010 Vancouver Games.

The Soviet Union team replaced Canada as the top international hockey team when they first competed in the 1956 Games.

Gathering and Evaluating Sources

Hockey is a big part of Canadian culture. Over 500,000 Canadians register each year to play organized hockey. Reread Chapters 1 and 2. What factors might have led to Canada dominating ice hockey? Using the Internet, research what happened in Canadian hockey between the 1956 and 1998 Games. What might have been the reason for Canada's absence on the gold medalist podium for 12 straight Winter Olympics? Use evidence you find to support your answer.

game, including the 2010 and 2014 Games. The only time the women didn't take home gold was in 1998 when they placed second, earning a silver medal. The men's team didn't take home gold again until the 2002 Games in Salt Lake City, Utah. Like the women's team, the men won gold during the 2010 and 2014 Games.

Soviet Union

The Soviet Union was founded in 1922 and began competing at the Winter Olympics in 1956. They dominated right away in men's ice hockey, winning nine straight medals, including seven gold. The Soviet Union was a huge and powerful country in Asia and Eastern Europe. It broke up into 15 separate countries in 1991. At the 1992 Winter Olympics, the Unified Team, which was made up of six of the former Soviet Union countries, won the men's ice hockey gold medal. After the 1992 Games, Russia, a former and big part of the Soviet Union, competed as its own team. Russia has won two medals since 1992: silver in 1998 and bronze in 2002.

The Chinese women's national ice hockey team made its debut at the 1998 Games.

Catching Up: China

China is hosting the 2022 Winter Games in Beijing and is gearing up to be a top competitor in ice hockey. The country has partnered with the Canadian Women's Hockey League (CWHL) in a deal that will establish a professional women's hockey team in China. The country, which has a population of over 1.3 billion, only has a little over 1,000 hockey players. China hopes the deal will not only help grow that number, but also promote hockey in time for the 2022 Games.

CHAPTER 3

Civics: Olympic Pride

Hosting the Olympic Games can be a big source of pride for the city and the people who live there. It gives the citizens a chance to show off where they live to the entire world. Through news articles and television, viewers learn all about the host country and city. Ice hockey is a sport that brings out the pride in Olympic fans. Fans travel from all over the world to watch their favorite players in sold-out Olympic arenas. Ice hockey usually gets the most television viewers, too.

Vladislav Tretiak, a former Soviet Union athlete, helped light the 2014 Olympic cauldron at the opening ceremony.

Most Watched

The 2014 women's ice hockey gold medal game between the United States and Canada had close to 5 million viewers in the United States. This was the most watched Olympic ice hockey game since the men's gold medal game at the 2010 Winter Olympics in Vancouver, Canada.

The most popular broadcast of the 2014 Winter Olympics in Canada was the men's ice hockey final between Canada and Sweden. Close to 9 million people watched Canada win the gold in a **shutout**. Canada scored three points and left Sweden with zero.

In Finland, the most watched event of the 2014 Games was the men's ice hockey bronze medal game between the United States and Finland. Close to 2 million viewers in Finland watched their country beat the United States 5–0, another shutout. The number of viewers was almost half of Finland's population. That was a lot of people tuning in!

Hilary Knight (US) chases Meghan Agosta (CAN) for the puck at the 2014 Games.

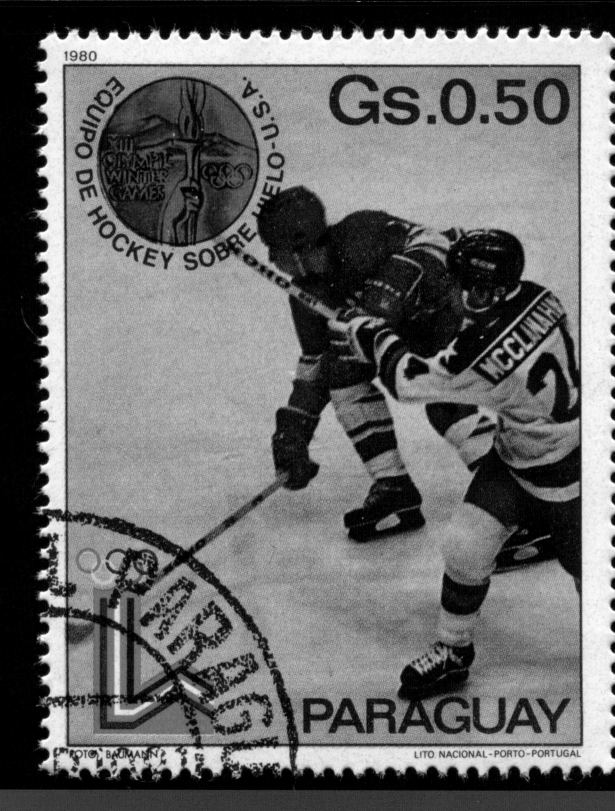

A postage stamp from Paraguay dedicated to the "Miracle on Ice" game.

"Miracle on Ice"

During the 1980 Winter Olympics in Lake Placid, New York, the US men's ice hockey team was facing the Soviet Union in the finals. Tension was high. Politically, the two countries did not get along. The Soviet Union, which had won five of the last six Olympic gold medals, was heavily favored to win. In a stunning victory, the US team came back from being down 3–2 to beat the Russians 4–3. The game is called the "Miracle on Ice." It couldn't be shown on TV live—it was aired hours after the game had actually ended. But it attracted 34.2 million viewers. It was the most watched ice hockey game ever by Americans. The United States went on to beat Finland 4–2 in the final for the gold medal.

Developing Claims

Do some research on the "Miracle on Ice" game. Why did the Russians and the United States not get along at the time? While you are reading about the game, look up what the Cold War was. Do you think the Cold War helped push the US team to win? Why or why not?

In 2016, Crosby was unanimously elected as the
Most Valuable Player (MVP) by the Canadian national team.

Golden Goal

More than 22 million Canadians watched when Canada won its second straight Olympic gold medal at the 2010 Games. Canadian star Sidney Crosby scored the winning "golden goal" in overtime to lead the Canadians 3–2 over the United States. At one point, at least 26.5 million Canadians were watching the game—this is 80 percent of the country's population! The "Golden Goal Game" is the most watched television sports event in Canadian history!

Economics: Ice Hockey Is Big Business

Hosting the Olympic Games costs a lot of money. Reports revealed that the 2014 Winter Olympics cost the host city of Sochi, Russia, more than $50 billion! This is why the Olympics wants the biggest and best stars to come and compete. If big stars aren't there to draw the crowds, cities won't earn back their money from **tourists** and fans.

No More Pros

As of 2018, the NHL will not let its professionals play. The league said too many players got hurt while playing in the past five Olympics. They also said having their players participate in the Olympics cost the league too much money. Since being

Fans celebrate Canada winning the gold at the 2010 Vancouver Games.

able to compete in 1998, there has been an average of 141 NHL players participating in the Winter Games every season. That is 141 players who are now no longer able to compete in the Olympics.

All About the Fans

Fans love their ice hockey, and TV stations broadcasting the Games want to give fans what they want. NBC, the channel that broadcasts the Olympics in the United States since 2000, is paying $963 million to broadcast the entire 2018 Winter Olympics, including the ice hockey games. All that money goes

Studies have shown that ice hockey fans prefer to see less fighting and more game playing.

Communicating Conclusions

Before reading this book, did you know much about ice hockey and the Winter Olympics? Now that you know more, do you think the NHL should or should not allow its players to play? Share what you learned with friends at school or with your family at home.

[21ST CENTURY SKILLS LIBRARY]

to the IOC. The IOC is the main organizer, promoter, and manager of the entire Olympics.

$963 million may seem like a lot of money, but to NBC it makes sense to pay. During the 2014 Sochi Games, an average of 21.4 million people in the United States tuned in to cheer on their favorite athletes. People also watched the Games using their laptops, phones, and tablets. During the men's ice hockey semifinal, over 2 million people live-streamed the event— a record-breaking number in the United States as of 2017!

Taking Informed Action

Do you want to learn more about the Winter Olympics and ice hockey? There are many different organizations that you can explore. Check them out online. Here are three ways to start your search:

- USA Hockey: Learn more about the US hockey team on its official website.
- US Hockey Hall of Fame: Discover how this organization preserves the history and recognizes extraordinary hockey moments.
- Olympics—Ice Hockey: Find out more about the history of ice hockey in the Olympics.

Think About It

Ice hockey used to be played in northern climates because the game was played outside on frozen ponds. Today, ice hockey is played all over the world. Canada still leads the way, with 624,162 players, the most registered players of any country in the world. South Korea, though, host of the 2018 Games, has seen its country's interest in the sport spike by 30 percent in the last few years. The country now has more than 2,000 ice hockey players. This doesn't compare to Canada's numbers, but it is still impressive. Do you think that hosting the Winter Olympics was the reason for the increased interest in this sport? Why or why not?

For More Information

Further Reading

Peters, Chris. *Great Moments in Olympic Ice Hockey.* Minneapolis: SportsZone, 2015.

Wallechinsky, David, and Jaime Loucky. *The Complete Book of the Winter Olympics.* Hertford, NC: Crossroad Press, 2014.

Waxman, Laura Hamilton. *Ice Hockey and Curling.* Mankato, MN: Amicus Ink, 2017.

Websites

The International Olympic Committee
https://www.olympic.org/the-ioc
Discover how the IOC works to build a better world through sports.

NBC—Olympic Winter Games: Hockey
www.nbcolympics.com/hockey
Learn even more about the previous and upcoming Olympic ice hockey events.

GLOSSARY

amateurs (AM-uh-choorz) athletes who don't compete for payment

playoffs (PLAY-awfs) a series of games after the regular season ends that determine which two teams will compete for the championship

professional (pruh-FESH-uh-nuhl) getting paid to do something others do for fun

puck (PUHK) a black disk made of rubber used in ice hockey

shutout (SHUT-out) a game in which one side fails to score

tourists (TOOR-ists) people who are traveling for pleasure

INDEX

Agosta, Meghan, 21
amateurs, 8–9, 26–27

Canada, 6–7, 10, 12–15, 20, 21, 25, 30
China, 16, 17
Crosby, Sidney, 24–25
Czechoslovakia, 8

fans, 18, 20, 25, 27, 29
fighting, 28
Finland, 20, 23

"Golden Goal Game," 25

hockey
    economics, 26–29
    geography, 10–17
    history, 4–9
    Olympic medals, 11, 12, 15, 20, 23, 25, 27
    organizations, 29
    tickets, 5

Knight, Hilary, 21

"Miracle on Ice," 22, 23

National Hockey League (NHL), 7, 8, 9, 26–27

Russia, 13, 15

South Korea, 30
Soviet Union, 8, 14, 15, 19, 23
Stanley Cup, 7
Sweden, 20

television, 18, 20, 23, 25, 27, 29
    See also fans
Tretiak, Vladislav, 19

United States, 7, 10, 11, 20, 21, 23, 25, 29

Winter Olympics, 4–5, 6, 14
    Canada (2010), 13, 15, 20, 25, 27
    China (2022), 17
    civic pride, 18–25
    Japan (1998), 6, 9, 12, 15, 16
    Lake Placid, NY (1980), 23
    organizations, 29
    Russia (2014), 4, 10, 11, 12, 15, 19, 20, 21, 26, 29
    South Korea (2018), 27, 30
women, 6, 9, 11, 12, 15, 16, 17, 20, 21